Spirit Guides

Rosemarie Koch

Houston
2019

For JFB 1941-1985

Copyright © 2019 by Rosemarie Koch
All rights reserved. This book or any portion thereof may not be reproduced or used in any manner or media whatsoever without the permission of the publisher or author except for the use of brief quotations in a book review or academic essay.

First Print Edition, 2019

ISBN 978-1-7323381-6-6

Brighten Press
Houston, Texas

info@brightenpress.com
www.brightenpress.com

Cover painting: William Baxter Closson, *The Angel*, ca. 1912.
Author photo and styling by Allison Goetz.

Spirit Guides

Contents

42   1

A Course in Spirit Guides   45

The Medium's Day-Book   69

Postscript/47   81

About the Author   105

42

*The cistern contains: the fountain overflows
One thought, fills immensity.*

— William Blake

i.

How many bones are there
in the body? How many broken, bruising,
calcifying?
Myself not in her bones, but of them?

Across the span of twenty-eight,
how many
dissemblings
of Mother?

ii.

First brush with magic:
a celadon bowl
filled with water
that I whip with a spatula
like a clock's second hand.
My mother's hair rolled
on orange juice cans
and fastened with clips.

Second floor porch
fashioned of narrow
pine stilts alongside
railroad tracks.
There my father's
hunting dog
hunts rats.

iii.

February cracker afternoons:

delicate trace French molding,
an eighth birthday party remembered.

Shoeprints left on snowy sidewalks,
the bone-china saucers
of all who came and went.

iv.

My grandmother recalling Lit Brothers
Department Store, and the free
trims for hats,
there my mother and her sister,
dressed in matching stripes,
sitting then for the lens, but now
both dead.
Their child selves rest
in a pearlized frame above
the front-porch switch.
Sharp as cut paper.
Fleeting as breath.

V.

Context for this:

If my great-grandmother fixed
to her hair the whalebone pins
and comb. If she unraveled
from her bombazine dress.
If she told the story of how
her husband picked up his lunch, only
to never come back.

vi.

Or, when there are too
many cloud-tops, it's as if
without sun you can hear
them whisper, it's as if
without sun there is nothing but
the way that the field of graves
in early snow looks,
washed by grief in mud tracks.

vii.

Even when three
hawks arc vertically over.
Cemetery in season,
visiting by road, visiting by pedal.
Geese eke their way
through marble passes.
No moss years, nor colorful churchyard.

viii.

When six hawks vault over
trees that curl atop
the unbound girls' hair of the crests
and apex of untended pines,
the whalebone pins
of time and nature.

ix.

January crows in hoods
etch across the sky
in a pitch more awkward, boats
on a glass-stained river.

X.

It's not about
crows' feet, turkey neck,
jowls that slack,
moles that change
and, altered, disappear.
Where before the scalpel
framed my beauty.
No creased ruffles of confusion, the skin
in selves of me far younger.

xi.

Now coming into the body
for seconds a day I am heavy.

xii.

If I look in a mirror:

see her at the edges of what I see
reveals like Bloody Mary in a shadow
at twelve. This standing before
mirrors six seven ten eleven.

Awaiting her appearance.

xiii.

The remembrance of my mother
doesn't crinkle and splash
in stolid marble like an ecstatic
habit of Avila. It is not touched
by God, is no Saint
Teresa by Bernini.

xiv.

My mother's face of cloud
and crumbling bones
across the broad sky down
the slope of the cemetery's
main entrance.
Off a suburban underpass.
Eight miles north of the city.
I long ago played Montresor.
In May and again in September.
I bricked her off.

XV.

Her maternal
grandparents rest amid the same staid
fence. That decision sat
with someone else,
in nineteen fifty-three
and nineteen sixty-one;
their sites are sinking.
Who outlived whom.
A man who on film was always laughing.
The smart cap of the dairy.
Her rolled-down stockings
and bright babushka.
I never knew them.
Natural causes.

xvi.

On the same angle of the field
I chose when I was fourteen.
Like all decisions important
to me always, I decided in an instant.
This is a hill, I thought.
And here is a tree she would know.

xvii.

Bough that dipped
like the wrist of a girl
accepting a dance.

xviii.

Visiting, I call it,
this subtle pilgrimage that shows
no timestamp. I tilt my face up
to the hawks.
That same tree is heavy now.
It creaks, and as I sit, I think:
I am crushed
under the weight
of this.

xix.

After twenty-eight years,
does anyone still feel
the pound and shard
of their heart, fragments
of a forgotten item?
Even if all journeys end at
churchyards and cathedrals.

XX.

Just two more years and they say
I will be her. Look at the literary
precedent of arriving at any sort
of predestination.
Protagonist in a kind
of symbolic trouble.
The forties intrinsic.

My twenties: preoccupation in
caged wrought iron.
My thirties of my own
small daughter.
Milk and panic.

xxi.

Try to make sense of it.
The mad, perverted
dash of dance floors
and fads and plates
of bacon — daughter
and the television.

xxii.

I went with her every week
from when I was eight.
That makes her thirty-seven.

Her hard veins
and the poison they pumped in.

First frozen yogurt
with coconut and chips.

Driving home, the market.
Squid for calamari
and a pinprick.

xxiii.

Antique row easel
carved "C," instant
relatives — no one we knew.
Their crepe wrists
accepting a dance,
eyes of blackened *cartes de visite.*

Where did the sickness come from?
That held the frozen pose
at twenty-nine.
The half-framed easel.

xxiv.

My grandmother would never
accept. I stood
having my hair brushed
without flinching
on my mother's behalf.

Radiation, therapeutic for skin. Oral
thrush and seagulls. Move to where
chlorophyll is bricked off by the sea.

XXV.

June. Seventh grade
eighth period *Tom Sawyer*.
Broken hip after aerobics
rendered her bones unequal.
Tears in the basement laundry.

xxvi.

I often see her
kicking me out of the car
almost at the intersection
of Five Points, the one
with the Baptist church
I could see from our bathroom window.
I have tried on a bikini.
I can't hear myself talking.

xxvii.

I flip to the last animation sketches, see
myself walking, flipping
pages to the hospice shuttle, the grandmother
next to me noting
the arrival of
Jewish New Year,
the grandmother
praising no rain.

xxviii.

Another woman, name unknown,
with half-grown sons also
was leaving

on the other side
of the plastic curtain.
One son studied
engineering, the baby-
blue vinyl chair, his eyes red.

This woman who was awake
along with my mother
at the three-week beginning

answered
when my mother
was ending.

xxix.

Before the last cancer:
a handful, tricyclic/MAO inhibitors.
With a glass of water.
Picasso face in the marbled mirror.
Now they'll only write at once for sixty
benzodiazepines.
I only took them to sleep.
My vanity.
I don't blame her.

XXX.

She didn't trust
his service revolver.
The death
wish seldom works, the cry
for help, the imagining
the dour MIDI Brandenburg
Concerti of one's funeral.
Faded white gladioli.

xxxi.

I think Death after
sleeping beside her
twelve summers was
no longer loud enough
to call her.
Daisies I brought dried out.
Late summer window.

xxxii.

Trace from that lost space
of twenty-eight
generations ago of carnations.
Their bony spires
of leaf and stem
laid crosswise on a casket.
An angel quotes *Hamlet*.

xxxiii.

For three years I didn't cry.
To organize flowers.
To braid grass
for a crevasse. To sculpt a bridge.

xxxiv.

They were and are not mine.
With hands of chalk
I climb them.
Count the platforms
of her scaffolds.

XXXV.

If I asked my cardsharp uncle
he would laugh.
Every Christmas
scarves and gloves.
I wondered why
they ever bothered.
He too
seven years after my mother.

xxxvi.

Nineteen seventy-eight's gift,
the grandfather clock.
The cornflower bowl.
Its glass frame broken.
My brother rescued it
like a body at sea.
The moon's phase frozen.

xxxvii.

My father, nearly remarried,
wanted her to pass at home.
She refused and instead
chose plastic and strangers
and the scented affront
of Pine-Sol and urine.

A curtain with tracks
could be pulled around
the whole arrangement.

xxxviii.

At the news,
my brothers cried.
They'd never now.
Their backs of flannel plaid shuddered.
Platitudes and bluster.
Trace and dismantle
the pins.

xxxix.

On the ground where I stand
stained green to the chlorophyll
reaches, this earth
of crumbled bones, falling off
miles away at the bending water, feeding
for a season the bending tree, the drape
of twenty-eight years of leaves.
Creak of détente or surrender.
I am of the frail
twigs of nesting birds.
Geese and deer in the horizon's
grass, treeline of locusts' purr.
Here hawks sweep
both low and distant.
Last year's nest. Forgotten paper.
Squirrels worrying frayed ribbon.

xl.

The matrilineal Lakota
and her whalebone pin
presides over the hallowed welcome.
She had long black hair.
Age itself could not defeat her
nor the stories of the ruined
Boston husband.

This is the ancestral gathering.
These are the impossible mosaics
that proliferate not by shattered glass
or fastening. They are the facets
of everything that was and is,
the essential tableaux
of whispering and release.

All one side of the curtain.

xli.

On the other
I plant portulacas
because it is almost their season.

Later the praying mantis
finds her way into the lavender
next to the cracked concrete.

A small garden
eclipsed by a rose
the size of a wingchair.

They avoid the mowers
simply by lifting
their nodded heads away
from the greased silver blades.

Up close to the edges,
pebbles flung into the hydrangea.

xlii.

My mother's
pink terrycloth penumbra:

she gardened a brick terrace
alongside a basketball hoop.

The drape of the Japanese maple,
the impossibly florid dogwoods
shedding pinched petals.

And row upon row of portulacas:
like children in a classroom
waiting, orderly bright bursts
of apricot and yellow

stronger than
a final diagnosis, and
past a mother's or a daughter's
season.

A Course in Spirit Guides

On subjects of which we know nothing, or should I say Beings . . . we both believe and disbelieve a hundred times an Hour, which keeps Believing nimble.

— Emily Dickinson

One

I broke
and I broke and I
broke and I broke
and broke again and again
and every time
I broke, I broke
a little less.

I feel the power ground
down in a shaft of light
on the blacktop's
span and I now
know who's near.

Cranberry ice and lime
and sweep
of parquet grace.
What I heard instead.
Your head tipped back.
Night fields. *Tempus fugit.*
Another glimpse:
chimera that
looked so much
like you, alas —
your face in relief,
leaves
speckle moth
streetlamp dark.

Picture the cracked
and broken
windows on a
vestibule that knew,
a half century ago,
a certain glamour:

the whole perambulating
scene of the days
when women wore
pumps and rayon
and everything was
because of the war.

Two

The first wore
a poncho from
her mother.
In her small hand,
she carried a hamster.
She wrote something
he couldn't read.
But it still mattered.

Was she a small woman?
Yes. She fell apart
in my arms, but
it took her two weeks.
Was she red-haired?
Yes. And she used to try
to scratch my face off.
She loved you.
No, I don't think she did.
She's still over
your right shoulder.

A temporal chasm.
Empty field
and two green
braided flashes.
Spirit had shown
the same in dreams.

You pulled her hair.
Just wrapped around
your hand like a scarf.
Every strand
prickled and tricked.
I'll be back.
No, you won't.
Yes, I will.
Orion's Belt.
The frosted dark.

Three

You know what happened, right?
I know you're a good man.
You know I insulted
his girlfriend
and he found out
and kicked me out
on Easter. Yeah?
I was there. You forget.
Then I slept on a ratty mattress
in a ground floor
by the boardwalk.
I couldn't even turn around
in the room.
I spent all my money
calling Mom.
When she died,
it was time to go home.

I go out and walk
some nights —
the stars fan bright
in their courses.
Sometimes the clouds
just crouch
above the streetlamps.
I feel somehow
bigger

            as if I could
change direction.
I pretend I'm in London
like Van Gogh
and can wander all night.

I have another life,
and then a third,
I suppose. There's an art
to traveling heavy,
then light.
I have met my shadow,
and she dances.

Four

Between realms.
There are men positing
theories counting
chances at gaming
tables holding the door
for other women refusing
pretending

           what they had was
better than what is
fixing an engine
with dad picking up
their mother's meds
making nice with
their wives when I know
what's inside and
operative. The tub comes right
through the joists
to the floor beneath.

My grandmother's house.
Purified by fire.
The old mill adjacent,
ancient labels and delinquents
and the gasoline where the next
day in the charred
disarray, the sniffer dog
smelled traces. . . .

    (Realized it reminded me
of my father,
Nutcracker tickets for . . .
no, not me. Stepmother ignored
my suggestions. Instead, fur coat, big
fancy dinner. Walked
right past me,
snubbed
my idea altogether.)

My father
said *You can't see
your mother.*

    I then asked:

*Will there be forty-eight
hours' notice on my
cemetery visits?*

So I had an affair.
Legerdemain and subterfuge.
I'd get the bus
as usual nothing out
of place, raisin
toast in foil pouch,
      get off at the clinic
      gates, meet my mother
      in her turquoise
      hatchback the shade of a wrap dress
      and she'd drive the rest.

Five

Like a room that steps down
to no light,

              the landscape
of the girl the family knew
was being starved, as they sat back.

She comes through
my channel now
without her name.

It happens all the time,
and is not mine.
Beaten with a cord
by her mother's man.
Flung against the radiator
like a second-hand lamp.
I saw her in the news.
I want to go back
and shield her
from the space.
I stopped breathing
too with the little girl
in the plastic bag.
I see the one whose
hair covered the hole
in her head from
the stepmother's broom
who got so sick
from secrets,
                one day she
was in class
and not the next.

I grew up somehow
to arrive at this place
despite or because of
all I told and hid.
And I know little girls grow
when they go too, so
that if an angel
arrives at five — soon
it's twelve.
I know they're not
tenacious
in wanting to remain
in our realm.
They see along with me
what came before
as filled with flames.
The pumpkin coach awaits.

I said a light appeared
above,
but I didn't know.
It may not be the same,
recalling, as it
really happened.
In such cases there's no
accounting.
It dilutes the
sad and lonely
jar of my best reference.

They sat on chairs
where they could watch
each other's faces
and she could listen
about Somali pirates,
stages, and lost linen.
Mirrored fragments
amid bottled labels.
He didn't go. The rose
inside her head
twined and twisted.

I can communicate
with the dead now.
*Ask them who
wins the Army-Navy game.*
They won't tell you that.
They only say
they love you.
They only say
things change.

I saw Death once.
She wasn't grand.
She hung beneath. She knelt
next to the space.
I felt first relief, then
a tunnel of grace.
Her underground weight like the subway
hurtling past.

The Medium's Day-Book

We rested again and again.

— Dorothy Wordsworth

No potions: just the seasons
and no tools, no eye

of newt, no petals except
when one incantatory midsummer
in my garden and shifting
terracotta pots, the
scrape of patio concrete,
sepia and pottery, insects
beneath, their bower
of flora.

Jimi Hendrix
mosaic from a wall,
his sequined eyes
squint straight past some horizon.

The woman in the narrow
shoes totters down
a slope, refusing
my help.

Like that.
To have the straight
intent of a chariot.
To have it fall
overburdened — flat.

This is the change-artist's
lot: to know that you span
realms and sometimes wish
you spanned a blink.

To have a bird be simply
wings and bones and not
a voice that speaks
through a void
you hear.

Some compact
image of a self
aligned in geometry
defined by solfeggio
harmonics instead

of flesh that
strains with the
weight of everyone else.

The Bible warns against —
the authors knew how heavy a yoke,
how hard to keep track.

To be someone to whom
people come back.
When a dark sky
is only dark, and
not a stated intent.

A medium is not someone
to convince. We look beyond,
invite you back
no matter how empty
your pocket, look now
how full.

There is your childhood
expanse, brief measures.
Your feelings —
numb. We get beneath. Soon
you are a spring. Next
you are a river that
flows past.

Each wakes
in a certain space
of regret, that
a new day might equal
or surpass that which
rests.

Since that was a shed skin.

It is either
anguish or grace
to assume the face
of a thousand hearts,
the weight
of a thousand breaks.

I think of it like
glass from sand,
to shape, to shard.

To somehow reassemble.
A voice, a strength, an ache.

Postscript/47

You must excuse the laconic Style of my Epistle as this place is damned dull and I have nothing to relate, but believe me.

— Lord Byron

Dreams of the land of the
long white cloud
for three days only: only
I never made it there.
The flight was too fraught, and
there was too much
unexpressed.
Gave me his car to drive with
controls untouched to one side.
We left it behind.

Instead, we walked the lots at night,
joking with Irish boys.
They were callow enough
to be our sons.

Another man texts from the feast,
she's God knows where, she's always
a wraith. I can imagine her, though,
as I do. They come either
full-fledged or half-baked.
Her voice grates.

In the mansion named for the owner
of a single nineteenth-century year,
its spires sedate. I feel
something there, with the steady
persistence of rats. The
monochromatic flower beds.
Not solid enough
to be a ghost: more like the trim
of a gingerbread.

A Wednesday when
another one comes in:
I wanted to see you today.
Text me after work.

I did. He didn't answer back.

I think we should revert
to the stolid sense of lunch.
Everyone behaves. When my priest
writes, I go, and we pray.
Not saying the saints
didn't bring a moment
of deliverance.
The proof is in
the lance.

My daughter: the particular ache.
Does anyone know what it's like
to be subject to what is not
discussed?
Twelve psychoactive manipulates.
Dense. Hospitals and chaos.
Precise order abates.

I drive sometimes
down the road
I was born.
I see exact decades-old
replicas of myself, perambulating
in circles that never end.

In the falling
dark, deer pick through the verges
and sedge.

And where I progress past
the week I fled
and landed here
and slept.
And didn't leave the couch
until next. I'm left
with the same polemic
morass. While others inhabit
enchanted forests.

The land of make-believe
and its adherents.
I read a piece:
it provides
a secure and predictive
archetype in which
to insert all your lies.

So there they stay, apart and away,
sweatshirts and scarves like clan
standards. The rest of us mull
outside the gates,
fairy tales unrendered.

I have a point to make
with women who are trying
too hard and realizing
nothing.

    A.) Your jacquard curtains
    B.) Your abstract sculptures of nuanced
       couples without eyes
    C.) Your grand olde holiday display

You're no better off
ordering around *hubby.*
Keep rhapsodizing that trip
from the nineties.
Someone you know
told me that story.

You don't know,
trimming your pachysandra.
How I hold a lost garden of
all the things
I used to use
to cover the empty.

How they've moldered and gone.
How everything
has its time and age.

An especial refrain
from any trope that yearns back
to former days.

How dull your Stepford
live, love, laugh.
How contrived your cheering
by the square. How smug
your tattoos in Chinese.

Can we reduce the things
we know but cannot see
to wooden sculptures
in the den?

Consider when it all goes
as unplanned.

What tattoo then?

So many names,
so many kitchens I occupied
and dishes I dried, gone, dust, all.
That one pair of pantyhose your mom bought
when you were eight so you
could feel like a lady.
The pomade that looked
like a baby duck. The mob cap
of your eighteenth-century
obsession in kindergarten. In your late
forties, you still fall asleep dreaming
of canopies, of bed-curtains and jeweled
miniatures, boxes for snuff.

How the dancing
queen I was has transformed
to the woman who has wiped
the tears of a psychotic,
then gone to work.
Sincerely yours.

All the while the granolas,
the ketos and kombuchas,
the flowers I can't grow,
the epic adventures
of the bipolar,
the unravelings and gatherings,
the lost and wandering
penumbras of the souls
up to their necks with
the debts of the past —
here they rest.

I don't know where the easel went.
I don't know how I hear her voice
and the voice of so many others,
a pumpkin's hollow,
echoing in my ribs and chest.

I don't know how I will see another night
through so many nights — when all seeds
are left to chance.

Ghosts. In a house
of wood, casts,
cats, pink chests,
and forgotten recompense.

Sometimes like an outcast
or a refugee.
Just beyond this:
wind, free.

About the Author

Rosemarie Koch earned her BA in English and Spanish and MFA in Poetry from Arcadia University. She also spent a year in the British Isles and Europe gathering inspiration while studying at Lancaster University. She has taken numerous supplemental writing courses, including those offered by Rabbit Hill Studio, by the authors Emma Jensen and Cordelia Frances Biddle, and through the University of Wisconsin-Extension.

She has spent her professional career in teaching, design, strategic development, executive support, and operations in education.

Rosemarie has been published previously in *Lingerings*, *Stirring*, and *Snakeskin*.

Please visit Facebook.com/RosemarieKochAuthor.

 Brighten Press

The Power of Words to Enlighten and Entertain

With all the many other demands on your attention in the world, we appreciate you taking the time to read this book.

We welcome you to explore our growing list of titles, which we believe will inspire, inform, and illuminate while never losing sight of offering adult and young readers intelligent amusement, engaging analysis, imaginative storytelling, and a good laugh, a good think, a good cry, and a good time.

Please visit us at brightenpress.com.

www.ingramcontent.com/pod-product-compliance
Lightning Source LLC
Chambersburg PA
CBHW060459080526
44584CB00015B/1483